Table of Contents

Chapter 0 What is this book about?

This book highlights the key steps of the application for Permanent Residency of Canada through Express Entry. Using my own experience as a benchmark, I would like to inform you of possible pitfalls and how long each step can take. I will also include my own letters of verification from employers and financial institutions (i.e., Proof of Means of Financial Support), as well as two Letters of Explanation, which I submitted to CIC. This information is especially relevant to you if you are applying through Express Entry from the United States. Since I spent my pre-college years in mainland China and college years in Canada, I will also cover the process of acquiring Police Certificates from these two countries.

Although I will talk about my experience and scores for you to use as a reference, this book is NOT about tweaking parameters to accumulate more points under the Comprehensive Ranking System (CRS).

I will go over the documents that I was required to submit not in order of their appearance in the online application portal, but in order of descending preparation time. Please be aware that you may have a slightly different document list based on your individual experience. If you are not in the United States, the document preparation times may not be applicable to you. Remember this as a rule of thumb: start from the document that takes the longest time to prepare and finish everything on your part as soon as possible.

Chapter 1 Requirements

1.1 Language Proficiency Exams

For Express Entry, you are required to present valid test results for IELTS (English), CELPIP (English) or TEF (French). Unfortunately you cannot bypass this step even if English or French is your native language. Since you can earn points for each of the official languages, you may want to submit test results for both to secure more points under your belt. If I knew more French than Bonjour and Je m'appelle Ye, I would have totally taken a French test to boost my score. My results for the IELTS test were:

Overall	Listening	Reading	Writing	Speaking
8.0	8.0	9.0	7.0	7.5

These in turn gave me 130 points under "CRS – Human Capital – First Official Language Proficiency".

I am going to spend the rest of this section going deeper into the IELTS exam, so feel free to move on to the next section if you have already taken the IELTS or are planning to take another test.

The IELTS test is a paper based English proficiency exam which can be conveniently taken in most parts of the world. Citizenship and Immigration Canada (CIC) does not accept IELTS scores that are more than 2 years old. The cost of the exam in the United States is $230 USD. From the date of examination, it usually takes about 13 days for the scores to be released. In my case, I took the exam on Nov/19/2016 and the IELTS administrator signed my Test Report Form on Dec/01/2016 (12 days from the date of examination).

The exam has four components, listening (30 min), reading (60 min), writing (60 min), and speaking (11-14 min). An exam taker completes the first three sections in one seating with no official breaks in between. Most questions are either fill-in-the-blanks or multiple choices. In the speaking test, the exam taker is recorded while answering a series of questions selected by a certified examiner.

If I were to take the exam again, I would

1) For the listening section, maintain a good rhythm between listening to the audio and answering the questions.
2) For the reading section, do nothing differently. I am happy with my basic strategy of skipping most information and searching for synonyms and paraphrases to the key words that the questions asked for.
3) For the writing section, use academic English instead of colloquial English.
4) For the speaking section, be organized and formal; elaborate on the last few questions to the best of my ability.

If you are interested, refer to a more detailed description of my IELTS exam in the Appendix of this book.

1.2 Assessment of Non-Canadian Educational Credentials

Depending on your educational background, you may need to have your non-Canadian educational credentials certified by World Education Services (WES). According to WES's official website, the standard processing time is 20 business days, and a WES Educational Credential Assessment (ECA) report is valid for 5 years from the date of completion for CIC purposes. To evaluate two degrees from the same US institution, I paid $233.91 USD and submitted my assessment request to WES on Jan/03/2017. I was notified of the completion of my evaluation report by email on Feb/22/2017 (50 days from the date of request submission). However, CIC invited me to apply for Permanent Residency on Jan/11/2017. This means that an applicant needs only one post-secondary degree, Canadian or WES assessed non-Canadian equivalent (I have a B.Sc. in chemistry from a Canadian university).

My education-related score breakdown is

Criteria	Details
CRS – Human Capital – Level of Education	120
CRS – Skill Transferability – Education	25

Take-home messages for you:

1) The more non-Canadian degrees you decide to assess, the longer it may take for WES to process your request. If you are on a time budget, assessing your non-Canadian degrees should be one of your top priorities.

2) You can save time and money by avoiding WES altogether if your highest degree is from a Canadian institution or if you are confident that your profile is good enough without having to assess your higher non-Canadian degrees. However, I would use this strategy with caution if my degrees were from different disciplines. For example, if I had a B.Sc. in mathematics from the University of Wisconsin-Madison (US) and a Master of Public Policy from the University of Toronto (Canada), I would go the extra mile to assess my US degree unless I was absolutely sure that it added no extra value in anything else, e.g., skill transferability.

3) You can save time and money by assessing your highest non-Canadian degree only. Similar to 2), use this strategy with caution if you have non-Canadian higher degrees in different fields of study, e.g., an M.Sc. in statistics from the University of Minnesota (US) and a Ph.D. in epidemiology from the University of Pennsylvania (US).

4) A Canadian B.Sc. degree in the basic sciences gives you 25 points for skill transferability and 30 points for Canadian education.

Chapter 2 Build Your Express Entry Profile Online

You will be scored and ranked according to the information you provided regarding your education, work experience, language skills, and family members accompanying you to Canada. If you are a Provincial Nominee or have a valid Canadian job offer, you are not required to register for Job Bank. Otherwise you must do so within 30 days of your profile creation. The online application portal will then generate your detailed score breakdown, such as mine below:

Criteria	Details
Federal Skilled Worker	Met
Provincial Nominee Program	Not Met
Canadian Experience Class	Not Met
Federal Skilled Trades	Not Met
Overall Score	465
CRS – Human Capital – Age	110
CRS – Human Capital – Level of Education	120
CRS – Human Capital – First Official Language Proficiency	130
CRS – Human Capital – Second Official Language Proficiency	0
CRS – Human Capital – Canadian Work Experience	0
CRS – Spouse – Level of Education	0
CRS – Spouse – First Official Language Proficiency	0
CRS – Spouse – Canadian Work Experience	0
CRS – Skill Transferability – Education	25
CRS – Skill Transferability – Foreign Work Experience	50
CRS – Skill Transferability – Certificate of Qualification	0
CRS – Canadian Education	30
CRS – Arranged Employment	0
CRS – Provincial/Territorial Nomination	0
Express Entry profile effective date	December 21, 2016
Express Entry client expiry date	December 21, 2017

According to CIC, your profile will

> "remain in the pool of Express Entry candidates for one year from the day you get in. Citizenship and Immigration Canada regularly selects the highest-ranking candidates from the pool by inviting them to apply to immigrate to Canada as permanent residents. If you do not get invited after a year of being in the pool, your Express Entry profile will expire.
>
> - If you still want to come to Canada as a skilled immigrant, you will need to complete and submit a new profile.
> - If you meet minimum entry criteria, you will receive a new Express Entry Profile Number."

With an overall score of 465, I was invited to apply for Permanent Residency on Jan/11/2017. The lowest score invited on that round was 459.

After receiving an Invitation to Apply, you have 90 days to provide more details and submit required documents for your application. More specifically, you need to give an unbroken record of your history of the past 10 years, including addresses, education/employment/unemployment, travel histories, etc. You will first need to fill out an online questionnaire, which is a more extended version of the one you have completed to create your Express Entry profile. Based on your answers to the questionnaire, you will then be required to submit a list of documents.

Since you can come back and revise your answers to the questionnaire, do not waste too much time on it in the first go but use it as a guide to see what kind of documents you need to collect. For example, the questionnaire will ask you to list all of your addresses and the start and end dates of each for the past 10 years. In my case, I am not one of those who retain previous addresses. In order to be accurate, I went through the rigor of tracing past landlords, subletters, bank statements and utility bills. I emailed, texted, or called 2 individuals and 5 companies in 3 countries. Guess how I felt when I learned 28 days into this rigmarole that FBI's processing time for Identity History Summaries (i.e., the US version of Police Certificates) was 12-14 weeks?

Let me emphasize again: do not fuss about the questionnaire, fill out enough information to get to the list of required documents first, and perfect your answers to the questionnaire based on the acquired documents later.

Chapter 3 Document Collection

My document list consists of

- Education (diplomas/degrees)
- Employment Records
- Transcripts
- Poof of Means of Financial Support
- Passports/Travel Documents (Multiple)
- Family Member Proof of Status
- Proof of Relationship
- Proof of Medical Exam
- Digital Photo
- Police Certificates (Multiple)

In the following subsections, I will go over these items one by one in order of descending preparation time.

3.1 Police Certificates

3.1.1 CIC Instructions

"You must provide a police certificate for every country, region or territory, other than Canada, in which you have spent 6 months or more. A police certificate is a copy of your criminal record, or a declaration of the absence of any criminal record.

Example: If you visited, worked or lived in a country for two months, left for a few years, then returned for four months, that counts as spending six months there. In this case, you would need a certificate.

Police certificates are different in each country and territory and may be called police clearance certificates, good conduct certificates, judicial record extracts, etc. They are issued by police authorities or government departments and used by Immigration, Refugees and Citizenship Canada (IRCC) to determine a person's admissibility to enter Canada.

Certain countries will not issue a police certificate, or provide the certificate directly to you. If this applies to you please provide a letter of explanation in lieu of a police certificate.

You will be advised if you are required to obtain a police certificate for Canada.

Police certificates need to be a scan of the original police certificate(s) in color. Certified true copies, unauthorized copies, or visibly altered police certificates are unacceptable and will result in the application being rejected as incomplete.

Once you have applied for a Police Certificate from a country, it is beneficial to upload evidence that you have applied in order to ensure that your application is not rejected as incomplete (examples of proof might include payment receipts, tracking numbers, etc.)"

3.1.2 Identity History Summary by FBI (US)

If you have cumulatively spent 6 months in the US, you will need to acquire an Identity History Summary (IdHS) from the Federal Bureau of Investigation (FBI). As of April 2017, the processing fee is $18 USD per person and processing time is 12-14 weeks. The FBI does not accept additional payment to expedite your request. However, if you are a citizen or a lawful permanent resident of the US, you may utilize the expedited service of an FBI-Approved Channeler. For example, it takes 24 hours for Accurate Biometrics to deliver an IdHS after they receive valid fingerprints and a payment of $50 USD.

To obtain a set of your fingerprints, you may visit a law enforcement agency. In my case, I went to the sheriff's office of my local county, mentioned FBI and form FD-258 (the standard fingerprint form), paid $10 USD, and my fingerprints were collected by a fingerprinting technician within 20 minutes of my arrival. To minimize the number of visits to the law enforcement agency, I recommend submitting multiple sets of fingerprints to the FBI or an FBI-Approved Channeler.

If you decide to request your IdHS from the FBI, you need to pay by credit card, money order or certified check the exact amount of $18 USD to the Treasury of the United States. I recommend checking periodically whether your payment has been cashed. For a credit card, the transaction will appear on your statement. For a money order, you need to track the transaction online according to its serial number. For a certified check, you need to contact the issuing financial institution. In case your IdHS does not arrive by the submission deadline, I recommend that you

- include a copy of your credit card statement or
- request from the issuing institution an official proof of transaction or a copy of the processed money order/certified check

as part of your proof of application for IdHS. If you choose to utilize the service of a financial institution, you may need to plan ahead. For example, for a fee of $5 USD, Huntington National Bank takes 7 business days to locate the record of a processed certified check. For your reference, my proof of application for IdHS includes

Item	Time Cost	Money Cost
Receipt of Fingerprint Cards	N/A	N/A
Receipt of Certified Check	N/A	N/A
FedEx Tracking Record	N/A	N/A
Copy of Processed Certified Check	7 Business Days	$5 USD

I did not end up submitting the documents above since my IdHS arrived on time. Below is my complete application timeline

Time	Event	Day Count
Feb/09/2017	Fingerprints Collected	
	Certified Check Obtained	0
	Package FedExed	
Feb/10/2017	Package Delivered	+1
Mar/25/2017	Certified Check Cashed	+44
	IdHS Issued	
Apr/05/2017	IdHS Received	+55

This means that there were 44 days (inclusive) from the date of fingerprint delivery to the date of IdHS issuance. I guess it is far shorter than the officially announced 12-14 weeks because I had no prior arrest data as of 03/25/2017. In fact, my IdHS must have arrived in my mail box between Mar/29/2017 and Apr/05/2017, since I check my mails once a week.

One interesting detail regarding my certified check was that the teller misspelled treasury as "treasurey". I did not notice this small mistake until I had FedExed everything to FBI. Another teller at the bank later assured me that the check was very unlikely to be rejected since it was going to be processed manually. Believing that my IdHS would take 12-14 weeks, I actually hoped that FBI would write me a letter requesting a typo-free check, which I could subsequently include as another piece of evidence for my IdHS application.

3.1.3 RCMP Criminal Record Check (Canada)

On June/23/2017, two and a half months after I submitted my Permanent Residence application online, RICC requested me to provide an RCMP (Royal Canadian Mounted Police) certified criminal record by the deadline of July/23/2017. In response to this request, I collected my ink-and-roll fingerprints and mailed them to Commissionaires Identification Services in

Ottawa to have them digitize the fingerprints and submit them to RCMP. As of June 2017, submitting fingerprints through accredited fingerprint companies (a list of which at the bottom of this page) was the only way for individuals outside of Canada to submit their fingerprints electronically to RCMP.

Below is my preparation timeline for the RCMP criminal record check:

Time	Event	Cost	Day Count
June/23/2017	Request of Criminal Record Check Received	NA	0
June/30/2017	Fingerprint Obtained	$10 USD Each	+7
	Forms Filled for Commissionaires	NA	
July/02/2017	Package FedExed	Receipt Lost	+9
July/04/2017	Package Received		+11
July/07/2017	RCMP Criminal Record Issued	NA	+14
July/14/2017	Credit Card Charged	$310.75 CAD	+21
July/17/2017	RCMP Criminal Record Received	NA	+24

Below is my itemized receipt of July/14/2017:

	Net	HST	Total
Scanned Fingerprints - International	250.00	32.50	282.50
RCMP Fee	25.00	3.25	28.25
Credit Card			310.75

3.1.4 Notarial Certificates (Mainland China)

You need to have your local police office (派出所), to which your household registration record, or 户口, is tied if you are a citizen, issue your criminal record, which you will then have a certified notary translate into English or

French. Both the original copy and the certified translation are to be scanned and submitted to CIC.

3.2 Proof of Means of Financial Support

3.2.1 CIC Instructions

"If you are applying for permanent residence in Canada, you must provide an official letter issued by your financial institution indicating your financial profile. This must:

- list of all your bank (chequing and savings) and investment accounts, the account numbers, dates each account was opened and the balance of each account over the past six months,
- list all outstanding debts, such as credit cards and loans,
- be printed on the letterhead of the financial institution, and include your name and the contact information of the financial institution (address, telephone number and e-mail address)."

3.2.2 Suggestions to You

If you can conveniently visit a local branch of your financial institution, do so. It is much easier to communicate IRCC's requirements in person than over the phone or via email. My personal savings are scattered in three banks, two of which do not have branches in my city. For the one that I was able to stop by, a letter was made, printed, and signed under my eyes within an hour. I called and emailed the other two since I did not want to hop on a flight or long-distance buses. In both cases, the telephone banking representatives directed me to my home branches, both of which treated my request as a special case. One of the home branches insisted that I visit them or another branch to have my letter processed, while the other escalated my case and eventually had it approved.

Do not leave Letters of Financial Support until the very last minute. They certainly don't take 90 days, but you never know when you will need a few extra days or weeks.

Below I include the letters that I submitted to IRCC. Feel free to use them as templates in case your financial institution asks you for one.

[Letterhead]

[Branch Address]

[Branch Phone Number] [Branch Fax Number]

March 14, 2017

Immigration, Refugees and Citizenship Canada,

This is to certify the bank accounts of [Applicant Name] at [Institution Name].

Account Type	Account Number	Date Opened	Balance as of 03/14/2017	Average Six Month Balance
Checking	135792468	MM/DD/YYYY	$XX.XX	$XX.XX

Six Month – **Month End** Balances		
February	2017	$XX.XX
January	2017	$XX.XX
December	2016	$XX.XX
November	2016	$XX.XX
October	2016	$XX.XX
September	2016	$XX.XX

[Applicant Name] has no outstanding credit cards or any types of loans with [Institution Name].

Any questions or concerns, please contact myself, [Banker Name], [Banker Title], [Banker Phone Number] or [Banker Email Address].

Thank you!

[Banker Signature]

[Banker Name]

[Bank Footer]

[Letterhead]

[Branch Address]

[Branch Phone Number]

[Branch Fax Number]

March 21, 2017

Immigration, Refugees and Citizenship Canada,

This letter is to confirm that the information below that has been provided by [Applicant Name] is in fact the information pertaining to the accounts in which [Applicant Name] holds at [Institution Name].

Account Summary				
Account Type	Account Number	Date Opened	Balance of 03/21/2017	Currency
Savings	123 456	MM/DD/YYYY	XX.XX	USD
Checking	987 654	MM/DD/YYYY	XX.XX	CNY

Six Month – Month End Balances		
Month	Account 123 456	Account 987 654
Feb/2017	XX.XX USD	XX. XX CNY
Jan/2017	XX.XX USD	XX. XX CNY
Dec/2016	XX.XX USD	XX. XX CNY
Nov/2016	XX.XX USD	XX. XX CNY
Oct/2016	XX.XX USD	XX. XX CNY
Sept/2016	XX.XX USD	XX. XX CNY

[Applicant Name] currently has no outstanding credit cards or any types of loans with [Institution Name].

Sincerely,

[Banker Signature]

[Banker Name] [Banker Title]

[Banker Phone Number]

[Bank URL]

[Bank Footer]

3.3 Employment Records

3.3.1 CIC Instructions

"You must provide proof of work experience for your current job and for each past position you listed (in the questionnaire). Proof must include a reference letter from your employer and pay stubs, if you have them. The reference letter must:

- be an official document printed on company letterhead
- include your name, the company's contact information (address, telephone number and e-mail address), the signature of your immediate
- show all positions held while employed at the company
- include these details: job title, duties/responsibilities, job status (if current job), the dates you worked for the company, the number of work hours per week and your annual salary plus benefits.

You must scan all documents for this period of employment and save them as one file. (You must create a separate file for each period of employment.)"

3.3.2 Suggestions to You

Include not only CIC's instructions but also sample reference letters in your requests to your current/past employers. They may ignore your sample letters, but most likely they will refer to them hence reducing the possibility of missing important information, e.g., benefits. One of my past employers even copied my sample letter (see 3.3.4 Sample Reference Letter 2) verbatim.

Don't be afraid to remind the persons in charge of your reference letters. They are busy, and sometimes cannot tend to your needs immediately. Just be polite and let them know that you understand.

If you no longer retain your previous pay stubs, contact your employers' payroll departments or payroll providers. If they don't keep your past pay stubs either, consider using your tax forms as a substitute. If none of you, your employers' payroll services and payroll providers, and your tax preparer have copies of your old tax forms, you may want to try your luck with your country's internal revenue service.

For each of my current and past positions, I strived to gather the following documents

- Reference letter from employer
- Paystubs (multiple if I worked for the company for an extended period of time)
- W2 forms

Below I include the reference letters that I submitted to IRCC.

[Company Letterhead]

March 27, 2017

To Whom It May Concern:

I am pleased to provide this letter to verify [Applicant Name]'s employment at [Company Name].

Jobs				
Job	Date	Annual Salary	Hours	Responsibility
Dragon Tamer 2	Present	Salary 2	40 per week	To tame a variety of breeds of dragons (e.g., a few examples) within the organization
	05/DD/2016			
	04/DD/2016	Salary 1		
Dragon Tamer 1	MM/DD/YYYY			

Benefits				
Benefits	01/01/2017-Present	Period 1	Period 2	Period 3
Medical	Y	Y	Y	Y
Health 1	Y	Y	Y	Y
Tobacco	N	N	Y	Y
Dental	Y	Y	Y	Y
Vision	Y	Waived	Waived	Waived
Health 2	Waived	Waived	Waived	Y
Accidental Death	Y	Y	Y	Y
Business Travel	Y	Y	Y	Y
Employee Assistance	Y	Y	Y	Y

Please do not hesitate to contact me should you need additional information or have any questions regarding the contents of this letter. I can be reached by phone at [Certifier Phone Number], or by email: Firstname.Lastname@company.com.

Sincerely,

[Certifier Signature]

[Certifier Name]

[Dragon Taming Director]

[Company Footer with Company Address]

[Company Header]

[Certifier Name]

[Certifier Title]

[Certifier Address]

[Certifier Phone Number]

[Certifier Email Address]

[Certifier Fax Number]

[Company URL]

Feb 28, 2017

Dear RICC Officer,

I am pleased to provide this letter to certify that [Applicant Name] was employed by [Company Name] as a [Job Title] from MM/DD/YYYY to MM/DD/YYYY. Her main responsibility was to [Job Responsibilities]. This job took about X hours per week. [Applicant Name] received a one-time payment of $XX USD at the end of the dragon breeding season.

Please do not hesitate to contact me should you have any questions regarding the contents of this letter.

Sincerely,

[Certifier Signature]

[Certifier Name]

[Certifier Title]

[Company Header]

Mar 9th, 2017

To Whom It May Concern:

Re: [Applicant Name]— DoB: Day Month Year

Verification of [Job Title] [Start and End Dates]

Dear RICC Officer:

As [Certifier Position] at [Company Name], I am writing in behalf of the Canada Permanent Residency application of [Applicant Name], to verify that [Applicant Name] was employed as a [Job Title] in the Division of [Division Name] at [Company Name] from [Start Date] to [End Date]. Her [Position] covered room and board for the entire duration of her stay, plus $X.XX per hour for hours worked in excess of XX hours per week. On average, [Applicant Name] worked XX hours per week.

[Applicant Name]'s main responsibilities included feeding baby dragons until they become too dangerous to approach, and offering hospice care to dragons who are terminally ill.

Thank you in advance for your consideration. Please do not hesitate to contact me should you need additional information or have any questions regarding the contents of this letter. I can be reached by phone at [Certifier

Office Phone Number] (o), or [Certifier Mobile Phone Number] (m); or by email: firstnamelastname@company.com.

Yours sincerely,

[Certifier
Signature]

[Certifier Name]

[Certifier Position]

[Company Footer with Address, Phone Number, Fax Number and URL]

[Company Header with Address]

February 20, 2017

To Whom It May Concern:

This letter is being sent to verify the status of [Applicant Name] in the Division of [Division Name] at [Company Name]. From [Month Day, Year] through [Month Day, Year], she was employed in the positions of Dragon Feeder and Dragon Trainer, as follows:

m/dd/yy – m/dd/yy, Dragon Feeder, salary of $XX/month

m/dd/yy – m/dd/yy, Dragon Trainer, salary of $XX/month

m/dd/yy – m/dd/yy, Dragon Trainer, salary of $XX/month

m/dd/yy – m/dd/yy, Egg Collector, salary of $X/month (additional job)

m/dd/yy – m/dd/yy, Dragon Feeder, salary of $XX/month

m/dd/yy – m/dd/yy, Dragon Trainer, salary of $XX/month

The duties of the Dragon Feeder job are to wash, chop and cook homegrown organic ingredients according to our divinely inspired Hatchling Formula. Hours per week for the Dragon Feeder job are X. The duties of the Dragon Trainer job are to monitor adult dragons during dragon-dragon combats and to assist them in research in the field of dragon-human combat. Hours per week for the Dragon Trainer job are XX. Duties of the Egg Collector job are to collect, sort and label eggs for 10 dens. Hours per week for the Egg Collector job are X.

[Applicant Name] also received reimbursement for her health insurance costs, which is a benefit offered to full-time employees in our division.

Please feel free to contact me if questions about [Applicant Name]'s appointment.

Sincerely,

[Certifier Signature]

[Certifier Name]

[Certifier Title]

[Certifier Phone Number]

[Certifier Email Address]

3.4 Medical Exam

3.4.1 CIC Instructions

"You require a medical exam. Learn how to get an upfront medical exam. In order to submit your online application, you will need to upload the information printout sheet or the IMM 1017B Upfront Medical Report form. Your doctor will give you one of these forms when you complete your medical exam.

If you cannot get a medical exam before the deadline to submit your work permit application, you may submit proof that you have scheduled an appointment."

3.4.2 My Experience

The nearest penal physician was 100 miles from my city. Since I didn't have a car, I had to ride a Greyhound bus, depart one night in advance, and sleep in a hotel overnight. Despite the travel, the upfront medical exam itself was only about 45 minutes. From my itemized bill below, you can see all the tests they performed.

Category	Cost (USD)
Comprehensive Physical Exam	$200
PA Chest X-Ray with interpretation	$100
Treponema Blood Test	$35
HIV 1&2 AB Blood Test	$40
Processing Fee	$50
Promotional Discount	-$25

The comprehensive physical exam included:

- Measurement of weight, height, and blood pressure; physician taking a photo of the examinee
- Urine sample collection
- Fundoscopy: physician inspecting the fundus of the eye using a fundoscope

- Vision: reading from an alphabet chart placed a few feet away (with prescription glasses or contact lenses on)
- Belly pressing exam
- Physician listening to internal organs using a stethoscope during normal and deep breathing
- Simple neurological tests including arm pushing, knee-jerk reaction, etc.

The promotional discount was offered to any examinee who completed all necessary paperwork before their scheduled appointment. The paperwork included:

- Basic information including date of service, name, date of birth, gender, country of birth, address, phone number, email, and immigration category (student, worker, family, etc.)
- Informed consent for HIV testing, which required the examinee's signature
- Acknowledgement of financial responsibility, which stated "the practice does not accept insurance and is not a Medicare or Medicaid provider" and required the examinee's signature
- A 2-page medical history questionnaire

Two surprises

- Neither did they give me any shots nor did they ask for my immunization records.
- My physician directly submitted my medical reports to CIC and notified me of the delivery via email.

My medical exam timeline

Date	Event	Day Count
Feb/10/2017	Appointment made	0
Feb/15/2017	Paperwork completed and emailed to physician	+5
Feb/16/2017	Receipt of paperwork verified by phone	+6
Feb/17/2017	Upfront medical exam performed	+7
Feb/22/2017	Examinee notified of the submission of the medical report to CIC	+12

3.4.3 Suggestions to You

If possible, complete all paperwork in advance. This gives you more time to ask questions and in turn saves you time during your exam.

If you haven't updated your eyeglass prescription for a long time, consider doing so and wearing more suited glasses/contact lenses for the vision test. It has nothing to do with fashion.

Most likely you will pay for the medical exam out of your own pocket. This, however, does not prevent you from mailing your bill to your insurance company. See what they have to say. Anything they reimburse you is better than nothing.

Don't forget to bring your passport with you.

You will still need to submit *something* under the "Proof of medical exam" category of the online application portal for the system to recognize your profile as complete and transmit your application. I submitted the email confirmation of the submission of my medical report and the receipt of my medical exam with the physician's signature.

3.5 Family Member Proof of Status & Proof of Relationship

3.5.1 CIC Instructions

Family Member Proof of Status

"You must provide a copy of your family member's Canadian Citizenship or Canadian immigration status document (e.g. Canadian passport, Permanent Resident Card, Study Permit, or Work Permit). Please provide a copy of both sides of the document."

Proof of Relationship

"You must provide proof of your relationship with your host or family member. This can include:

- a marriage certificate
- Statutory Declaration of Common-Law Union (IMM5409)
- a birth certificate
- an official document naming you as a parent
- a copy of the inside back cover of the inviter's passport showing the inviter's parents, if applicable"

3.5.2 My Experience

I was required to submit a *Family Member Proof of Status* and *Proof of Relationship* because I listed my uncle as a family member in Canada when I was building my online Express Entry Profile. I was not sure whether I did the right thing, but I did not want to jeopardize my application by omitting my family connection in Canada, not knowing what CIC's definition of honesty was. However, I felt extremely uncomfortable when the online application portal later prompted me to submit these documents. Who the hell, in their right mind, would ask for their uncle's government documents? I was very grateful that my uncle not only emailed me a copy of his Canadian document right away, but also worked with my mother to certify the sibling-daughter-niece relationship between the three of us.

3.5.3 Suggestions to You

If you also listed a family member in Canada, you will need to submit their Canadian Citizenship or Canadian immigration status document and provide sufficient proof of the said relationship between you and the family member. For Proof of Relationship, I submitted the following documents to CIC

- Government certification of the three-way relationship between my mother, my uncle, and me, indicating the government ID (i.e., passport) number of each individual
- Photocopy of the government IDs of mother and me

However, to acquire the government certification, my mother and uncle prepared the following documents (not submitted to CIC)

- The birth certificates of my mother and uncle, indicating common parents
- My birth certificate, stating my mother as a parent

Altogether, it took my mother and uncle about a month to finish preparing these documents.

3.6 Digital Photo

3.6.1 CIC Instructions

"Frame size

- The final frame size of the photo must be at least 35mm × 45mm.

- The photographs must show a full front view of the head and tops of shoulders, with the face in the middle of the photograph.
- The size of the head, from chin to crown, must be between 31mm and 36mm.
- Digital dimensions are often expressed in pixels or DPI (dots per inch). The physical dimensions in pixels must be at least 420 × 540.

Quality/resolution

If an existing photo is being scanned, the minimum resolution must be 600 pixels per inch.

File format

- The file may be submitted in JPEG or JEG2000 format.
- The final size of the image should ideally be 240 kB (kilobytes), but not less than 60 kB.
- The image must be in color (24 bits per pixel) in RGB color space, which is the common output for most digital cameras."

3.6.2 Suggestions to You

In the US, both Walgreens and FedEx can take instant photos satisfying the requirements above.

IMPORTANT: the photo requirements for the online application portal are DIFFERENT from those for passport submission (Chapter 5 Passport Submission).

As of April 2017, Walgreens was only able to burn digital photos into CDs. In other words, they were not able to email digital photos or transfer them to thumb drives. If you choose Walgreens, make sure your computer has CD slots or you have convenient access to a scanner.

Neither could FedEx email me my photo, but they copied it into my USB drive. Since I did not have any photos printed, FedEx decided not to charge me for printing. My final bill from FedEx was $0.89 USD.

3.7 CIC Instructions for All Other Documents

3.7.1 Education (diplomas/degrees)

"You must provide proof that you completed your post-secondary education. Examples of proof of education include a diploma and/or degree. Examples of post-secondary education are:

Trade/apprenticeship

- Training in a specific trade, such as carpentry or auto mechanics;
- Training in a profession that requires formal education but not at the university level (for example, dental technician or engineering technician); or
- Training not at the university level for which a certificate/diploma is awarded.

Bachelor's degree

- This is an academic degree awarded by a college or university to those who completed an undergraduate curriculum (also called a baccalaureate). Example: a Bachelor of Arts, Science or Education.

Master's degree

- This is an academic degree awarded by a graduate school of a college or university.

Ph.D.

- This is the highest university degree, usually based on at least three years of graduate studies and a thesis. Normally, you must have completed a Master's degree before a Ph.D. can be earned."

"You must submit a legible copy of your valid travel document which you will use to travel.

If you have a passport, you must provide a copy of:

- the page that shows your birth date and country of origin, and
- any pages with stamps, visas or markings.

If you do not have a passport and must use another travel document, it must be issued by a government and include your:

- name,
- date of birth,
- document number,
- citizenship or residency status,
- photo, and
- expiry date (if applicable)."

3.8 Letter of Explanation

3.8.1 CIC Instructions

"If you would like to provide more information about your application that you have not already provided, you can attach a letter of explanation to your application."

3.8.2 Suggestions to You

Before compiling your documents for final submission, make sure that everything you are about to submit is truthful, consistent with everything else, and compliant with CIC requirements. For example, below are a few things you need to check for consistency:

- The employment dates you entered in the questionnaire must align with the dates your employers stated in your reference letters.
- The salaries on your reference letters must match the numbers on your pay stubs.
- The balances of your bank accounts on your Proof of Means of Financial Support must be the same as they are on your bank statements.
- The contact information (i.e., physical address, phone number, and email address) of each of the certifiers for your employment history or financial support must be correct. If you decide to include business cards of your certifiers, the contact information on each card had better agree with the contact information on its corresponding reference letter/Proof of Means of Financial Support.

Below are a few examples of noncompliance:

- One of your past employers forgot to include the benefits of your position.
- One of your Police Reports cannot arrive by your submission deadline.

Correct any mistake, inconsistency or noncompliance as soon as possible. Otherwise explain yourself in a Letter of Explanation. Remember that it is your responsibility to ensure the accuracy and completeness of your application materials, not your employers' or financial institutions'.

When I was checking my documents for consistency, I realized that the phone number on my current boss's business card was wrong. To make my application correct and consistent, I decided not to include any business cards even though I had asked for them.

When I was checking my documents for compliance, I noticed that one of my certifiers forgot to include her email address. This minor neglect escaped my attention when I received the letter from her for the first time, because the letter looked very much the same as my sample letter which did have a bracket for email address. Given my deadline and the time of mail delivery, my safest solution was to write a Letter of Explanation (see below) but not to have her reissue the letter. For the second Letter of Explanation, please see Appendix.

3.8.3 Sample Letter of Explanation 1

Letter of Explanation

[Applicant Address]

April 8th, 2017

To Whom It May Concern:

The email address of [Certifier Name], the [Acronym of Institution Name] employee who helped prepare the Proof of Means of Financial Support, is CertifierName@institution.com. An earlier communication between Ms. [Certifier Last Name] and [Applicant Name] is included on the next page for reference.

Sincerely,

[Applicant Signature]

[Applicant Name]

Chapter 4 Compile Your Documents for Submission

There are many ways to merge, rotate, and compress pdf files. If you decide to utilize an online pdf platform, make sure that your documents stay private and are deleted once your task is complete.

I paid $5 USD for one week's access to Sejda's (https://www.sejda.com/) online PDF platform. They do a good job at rotating, cropping, merging, compressing and deleting pages of pdf documents. However, they are unable to perform multiple functions at once. For example, in order to rotate one of my diplomas and then merge it with my other diplomas, I needed to perform rotation and merger in two separate steps. More specifically, I had to reload the rotated document for merger. Another inconvenience is that they have a size limit (I don't know exactly how large) for compression. I had to use another online pdf compressor (https://www.pdfcompress.com/) for some of my 2MB files.

Chapter 5 Passport Submission

Once your application is approved, RICC will request you to submit
(photocopies of) your passport and two photographs of yourself and your
accompanying dependents. Because the required dimensions of the
photographs are so specific, you may need to hire a commercial
photographer. Make sure that you do everything right in the first place, since
the Visa Application Centers do not hold application materials for more than
5 business days (Yes, I learned it the hard way).

Event	Date	Time Elapsed
Application Submitted	Apr/08/2017	0 Day
RICC Contact for Additional Information	Jun/23/2017	+ 76 Days
RICC Contact for Passport Submission	Aug/31/2017	+ 145 Days
PR Status Approved	Oct/04/2017	+ 179 Days

Appendix

A.1 My IELTS Exam

The Listening Test

The listening test had four audios.

The first audio was a telephone conversation in which a woman inquired about the classes offered by a local education center. At the very beginning of the audio, I was asked to write down the street name of the center. The center representative pronounced each alphabet once and only once, without illustrating them using common names such as "m as in Mary". Therefore, you should be extremely vigilant whenever you hear "let me spell it out for you". The entire conversation covered two to three classes, for each of which at least one of the three aspects, subject matter, time of instruction, and age group (i.e., children vs. adults), was discussed. For the carpentry course, there was specifically a question asking what was not included in the course fee. The answer was the cost of course material, wood.

The second audio was a park ranger/tour guide speaking about different features of a resort center. There were four multiple choice questions and a map with about 5 to 8 missing landmarks which I had to fill in based on the directions given by the speaker. The only multiple choice question which I still have an impression of asked "which one of the following machines takes coins". Choice A "public telephones" was the first machine introduced. All I was certain was that the park's telephone booths used to take coins, but they were replaced by newer models, whose features I missed when erasing Choice A as my answer. The speaker also mentioned "… our laundry machines take one dollar pieces. You can get change from the Visitor Center." This made "laundry machines" a very confusing choice for me, since I wasn't sure whether "one dollar pieces" meant one dollar notes or one dollar coins. (One dollar coins, although rare, are still in use in the United States.) On the other hand, the map filling exercise was relatively straightforward.

In the third audio, a woman, presumably a secretary, gave a young man, presumably a customer facing employee, his boss's evaluation of his performance on the job. The conversation went back and forth between the boss's assessment and the man's self-evaluation. There were a total of 4 multiple choice questions. Quite naturally 2 of them asked about the boss's opinion and the other 2 asked about the man's own opinion. I remember that 1) the boss commented that the man was very bright and a source of good suggestions and that 2) the man himself said that he wanted to build more confidence when speaking to customers in French.

The last audio was a short lecture on an endangered bird species in Great Britain (whose name I forget). The lecture addressed the reasons for the bird's population decline from the 1800's to the present day. In the past, the bird's beautiful feathers were highly sought-after decorations. In modern days, its food supply (i.e., fish) diminished and natural habitat shrunk due to human activities, e.g., the release of chemicals into water. It was also noted that the fish, which was the bird's primary energy source, lived in between weeds. Can you guess whether the audio mentioned the British Government's conservation efforts? All questions pertaining to this audio were fill-in-the-blanks.

The Reading Test

I only remember the first and the last reading materials.

The first reading material consisted of introductions to 6 museums labeled from A to F. The entire A4 exam paper was divided to 6 blocks, within each there was a 5-8 sentence introduction to one museum. The questions consisted of 6 descriptions, 5 of which I remember (the exact wording and order may vary):

1) This museum was built on a historic site.
2) The exhibits in this museum were made from a single material.
3) This museum has audio collections.
4) This museum owns a war related artifact.
5) This museum displays objects belonged to the royals.

The exam taker's task was to match the descriptions with the museums.

The second or the third reading material was about a unique store which sold unusual merchandise only to its registered members. There were about 4 multiple choice questions associated with it.

The last reading material was a scientific introduction to laughter. It was divided into 4 sections, each covering a unique aspect of laughter and requiring the reader to select its title from 4 possibilities. Some of the earlier sections touched on the rhythmical contractions of the respiratory system in other animals, e.g., birds and higher primates. The last section discussed how people in different age groups may laugh for different reasons. More specifically, teenagers sometimes laugh to express their individuality and defiance of social norms. The entire article was filled with scholars' names and quotes, with some of the names appearing in multiple locations. There was a question that asked the reader to match the names of the scholars with their academic beliefs.

The Writing Test

The two writing tasks were given to and collected from an exam taker at the same time. This means that they could potentially adjust the time they use for each task, provided that the total writing time is not more than an hour. My tasks and responses were (and I paraphrase):

"Write a letter to a friend to describe a piece of technology that you recently purchased and state the reason(s) why you would/would not recommend the product to your friend."

My response:

Dear xx,

As you already know, I purchased a Blue Snowball condenser microphone from Amazon two weeks ago to kick start my online education business. The gadget comes with a stand and a USB cable, which can be hooked up to any computer, mac or pc. The microphone picks up sound from all directions. The only thing you need to do is to experiment with the distance from the microphone when you record. My optimal recording distance is about 12 inches. The microphone is very sensitive, and it may pick up computer fan noise and echoes in the room. Don't record in your living room since it has too much reverberating sound.

I really enjoy the microphone's crystal clear sound and cute little head. Since I know you are recording podcasts directly to a sim card instead of to a computer, computer fan noise wouldn't be a problem for you. Why don't you stop by my place and test it out this evening? You can then decide whether you want to invest from there.

Sincerely,

∞

"Some people think that students should be a little afraid of their teachers so that they can learn better. Other people think that teachers should be friends to their students. Which side do you agree with?"

Since I cannot completely recall my response to the second task, I will briefly describe my writing process below.

Immediately after receiving the writing tasks, I spent 5 minutes on a bathroom break. I used the brisk walk to brainstorm. My Blue Snowball condenser microphone, which I purchased a week prior, came to me effortlessly for Task 1. Although I honestly believe that the best learning experience is created when teachers and students totally accept and support each other, I wasn't able to come up with any supporting reasons even after I sat down on my writing chair. Since I didn't want to lose any more time, I picked up the pencil and started to write anyways.

For the following 40 minutes, my paper was gradually filled by an essay with the following starting paragraph:

"'Some people think that students should be a little afraid of their teachers so that they can learn better.' Who are 'some people'? If they are teachers, they must be Nazis who enjoy dictating more than teaching. If they are students, they must be brainwashed submissives who have not the slightest clue what true learning is like. Having completed my primary and secondary education in mainland China then college and graduate studies in North America, I have experienced the best and worst of both worlds. Let me reveal this sacred truth to you – human beings cannot learn when they are afraid."

I spent the second paragraph touching on the fact that the fear processing center of the brain (i.e., the amygdala) should be turned off in order for the CEO of the brain (i.e., the prefrontal cortex) to function at its maximal capacity. During the exam, I was not able to recall the correct spelling for either anatomy. I briefly described their functions as fear processing and higher reasoning, labelled them as "fear center" and "CEO", and asked the curious grader himself/herself to Google for the correct names.

As soon as I finished the second paragraph, I found myself running out of supporting evidence again. There was a 30-second pause when I tried to conjure statistics and facts. The attempt failed so miserably that I couldn't even think of a single case when someone's learning experience was jeopardized by a cringeworthy teacher. "Fuck it! Let me simply describe to my reader how the learning experience feels like when the learner is loved and accepted by the teacher." I thought to myself.

Shortly afterwards I found myself writing "Learning becomes an open-ended invitation from the limitless unknown. The learner feels that the boundary between the Self and the Unknown begins to blur and time seems to stop. This state of deep learning can only be paralleled by extended meditations and orgasms. Having tasted something like this, who wants to revert to the pupil-disciplinarian model where everything is about ego, punishments and rewards?"

Shocked at what I wrote, I immediately went back, erased "and orgasms" and re-wrote "and orgasms". My mind travelled to a time when Marianne Williamson, a renowned American spiritual teacher, spoke on my computer screen: "Good sex, what the body can do. Great Sex. What body?" then the whole audience laughed. If sex is indeed a deep spiritual experience, which people can use to transcend the matter-consciousness barrier, then why should people have issues talking about it openly and shamelessly? Let me leave it there and see what happens...

There was approximately 15 minutes remaining in the writing test when I finished my third paragraph of Task 2. I used 11 minutes to write Task 1 (see above) and another 1 minute for the concluding paragraph of Task 2: "It is ridiculous to have teachers who think that they should be afraid of. It is the 21st century already, and we have learned enough to know that fear doesn't help us achieve anything meaningful. We should grow up and embrace a teaching model where teachers and students are friends."

There was only 1 minute left when I finished writing. This wasn't enough for me to proofread even though I wanted to. As I am typing now, I can still recall a few spelling errors, redundancies in language, and sub-optimal usages of words and phrases. I think these errors cost me at least 0.5-point worth of writing score.

The Speaking Test

Part I

Examiner: Do you like chocolate?

Me: No. Chocolate was not a common food when I was growing up. I don't like it because I'm not used to it. Maybe I am not acceptable (receptive) to new things.

Examiner: Have you ever given anyone chocolate?

Me: No. I don't like giving people perishables. I prefer to give them something that lasts so that they can remember me.

Examiner: Why do you think chocolate is so popular?

Me: Because of stupid commercials, who want you to believe that if you give someone chocolate, they'll like you in return.

Examiner: Have you ever taught someone?

Me: Yes. When I was a graduate student, I taught undergrads physical chemistry and general chemistry.

Examiner: Do you enjoy teaching?

Me: Yes and no. In the beginning it's always like "Wow I got to be on stage and I got so much attention". After a while it starts to get boring, with the same thing over and over again. Recycled platitudes, you know.

Examiner: Do you plan to teach in the future?

Me: I don't plan to teach unless it (what I teach) teaches me something in return.

Part II

Examiner: Can you tell me about a happy event, how you prepared for it, and whether it was successful?

I had 1 minute to prepare for the mini-speech and was handed a pencil and a small piece of paper to take notes. The pencil and paper were given back to the examiner at the end of the speech.

As my response, I spoke about a 3-day workshop that I attended in Las Vegas in the mid-October of 2016. I began with an introduction to the event host, Steve Pavlina, his personal development blog, and his experimental approach to life. I mentioned two of Steve's life-style experiments, raw veganism and polyphasic sleep, which were quite popular among his readers. In retrospect, the Steve Pavlina part of my response was too long, and I should have avoided using too many distracting terms like polyphasic sleep.

For the "preparation" part, I said (roughly):

"Preparation was relatively straightforward. All I needed to do was to register for the workshop online, book a flight and book a hotel. My only concern was that I had exhausted all of my PTOs (paid-time-off, which I didn't but should have explained) at the time. What if my boss wouldn't let me go? I hopped into his office and basically just announced 'I am flying to Vegas on Friday'. Guess what he didn't stop me."

It wasn't until when I was about to conclude did I realize that I had not said a word about the event's successful ending. So I said in a hurry, "The whole thing was a blast! I loved hanging out with like-minded people!"

Part III

Examiner: Do you prepare for work every morning?

Me: No. My job is rather mundane and boring. I am not looking forward to it.

Examiner: What about your colleagues? Do they prepare for work?

Me: I guess so, just by looking at their faces. They look miserable and stressed out whenever they prepare for something bad to happen to them.

Examiner: Why do you think people prepare?

Me: Because they have this illusion that they are safe after they prepare. Let's face it. There is no absolute certainty in this reality except our ultimate physical death. Why should we prepare? I usually look for synchronicities and follow impulses. Even for this exam, I am totally unprepared and just say whatever comes through me.

Examiner: Why do parents teach children to prepare?

Me: What to prepare for? Exams? Life?

(Awkward 3 second silence. I realized that if I didn't speak the clock would keep ticking forever.)

Me: Learning is bringing light into the unknown. It is a process completed by the learner itself. I don't believe that teachers or parents actually teach students.

Examiner: What about really young children?

Me: (Sighed) Learning is an adventure of self-discovery. The primary role of teachers and parents is to provide options. "Do you like this? Do you like this? What do you think will provide the best learning experience?" I don't believe in the pupil-disciplinarian model (Mind wandering to the writing task).

Examiner: Do you think you can learn to be organized?

Me: I don't believe that there is anything that cannot be learned. If millions of people are doing it, I don't see why I can't do it. The question is whether or not I want to be organized, and the answer is no.

Examiner: Do you think companies should take risks?

Me: I am not a business owner … yet…, I can't say for sure. Taking risks is generally a good thing. The universe will reveal previously hidden things when you take risks. (3 sec pause) Yeah… if you don't take risks, how can the universe reveal things that were previously hidden from you? (3 sec pause) Plus, taking risks is fun. Who says we can't have fun?

A.2 Summary Statistics of Express Entry Applicants

You can find the CRS score distribution of the most recent pool of Express Entry applicants here. I plot the results of May/12/2017 into Figure 1. The percentile of an invited candidate (assuming that there were 3,678 of them) was no less than 92.40%.

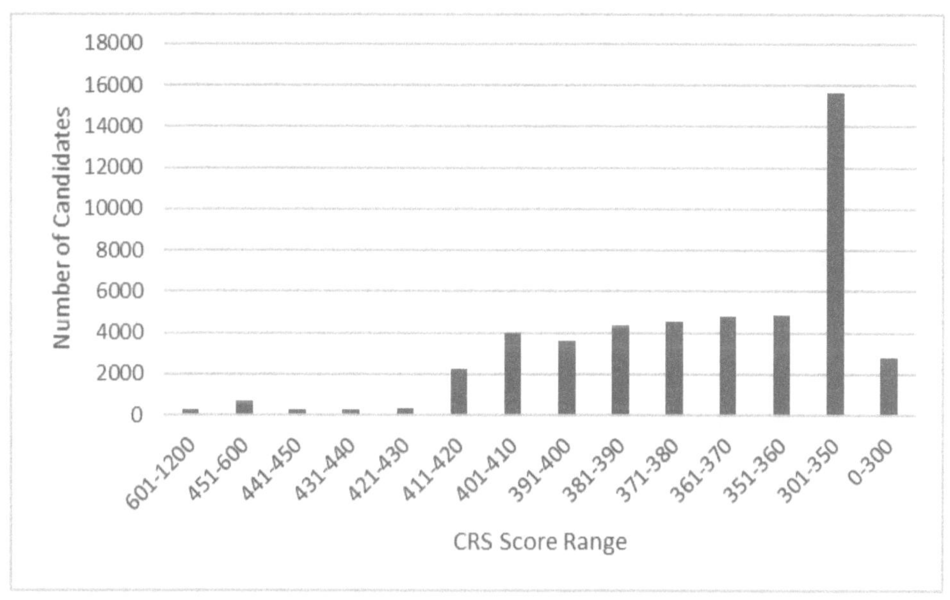

Figure 1. CRS Score Distribution of Express Entry Candidates as of May 12, 2017

You can find the number of invitations and the CRS score threshold for each of the historical rounds since Jan/31/2015 here, which I plot into Figure 2.

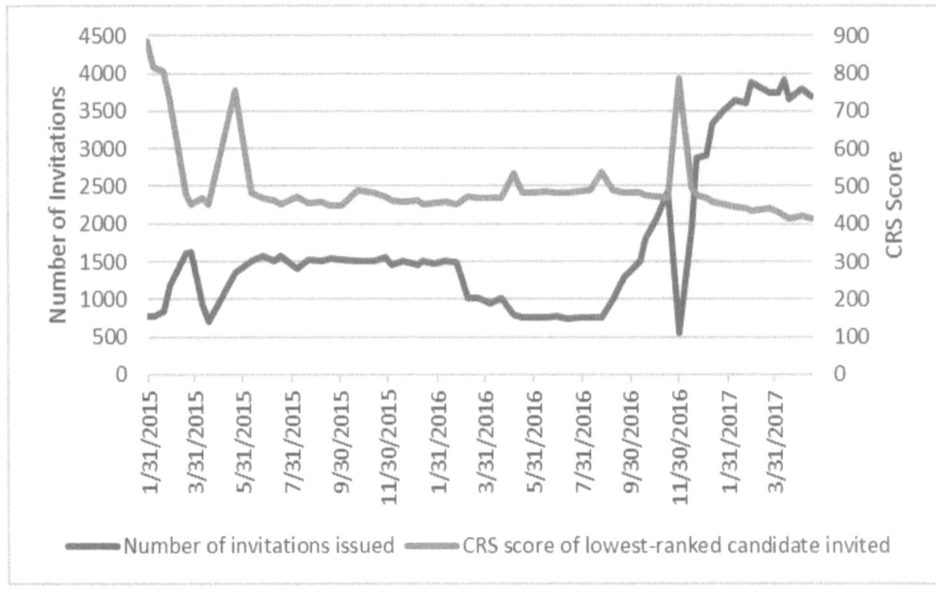

Figure 2. Historical Number of Invitations and CRS Score Threshold (Jan/31/2015-May/17/2017)

A.3 Sample Letter of Explanation 2

[Letter of Explanation]

[Applicant Address]

July 18th, 2017

To Whom It May Concern:

There is no expiry date indicated on the RCMP record. A date was randomly selected so that the online application portal would accept the record.

Thank you for your understanding.

Sincerely,

[Applicant Signature]

[Applicant Name]